Breathe In Daisy, Breathe Out Stones

Cindy Rinne

FUTURECYCLE PRESS
www.futurecycle.org

Library of Congress Control Number: 2016951494

Published by FutureCycle Press
Lexington, Kentucky, USA

ISBN 978-1-942371-16-8

For Cori

Contents

I.

A Ritual

Savory

Y vuelvo a verlo, y cada dia espero
And I come back to see him, and every day I wait.

—Pablo Neruda

I.

The north wind crashed
an ancient eucalyptus. This tree
was burned in the fire that burned her house.
The tree survived the ash.

Top branches almost touch the stream.
The tree whispers
that he longs to reach the sea.
She picks up a fallen branch
and decides to carry it there.

II.

Roots exposed, the eucalyptus
becomes a large nest. A lizard.
The spider spells
the word *salt*.

III.

The leaves blink like an eyelash.
Tell one another, *She is the one
we've been waiting for.* She listens
to the ghost of a stream—
and sees the burnt edges. Fallen
eucalyptus trembles and moans.

I am cracked open.

What must this be like? She observes
exposed shards stitched together. Frida
painted this image of fire.

IV.

She notices a flat space lined by trees. A family
used to live here and calm their baby in Spanish.

Duermase mi niño
Duermasme ya.

V.

A drought means leaves
and clusters of seed pods
hang on like brave warriors.

After resting on the ground,
the warmth of a blood-pulsed
hand stuns. A skeleton with angel wings
pedals by and offers
to complete the task. With the courage
of La Adelita instilled in her, she declares,
the promise is mine to fulfill.

VI.

The orange man rapes the
eucalyptus branches,
strips the skin with a curved blade,
and abuses the trunk. The cuts echo
like an exploding piñata. Niños laugh
as they win the prize.

She inhales
the sawdust. Sits on Diego's spine, trunk
slices flung like dice. Once a living cistern,
now time to weigh the heart—

a feather; aerial roots
graft to the web. The rainbow spider
spins the word *tides*.

VII.

Felling from the dead—
Borges wrote: *The eucalyptus trees*
bestow on the gloom their medicinal smell:
that ancient smell, spirals down to the tree's
beginnings, the first light. Death is cold.
Dios del mar is content
in his palace on the ocean floor.

VIII.

She discovers Castilian roses in winter like
the imprinted apparition of Guadalupe
born of cut flowers and of soil.

A Ritual

After *Woman with Sticks* by Ron Mueck

The nude woman,
muscles bulging, collects
mulberry sticks,
cut branches
left in her neighbor's backyard.
He will return to store them
in the cement shed
behind his
Bauhaus-style home.

I take them as donations
for my organic abstractions,
natural sculptures, she says
to herself.
The infinite sticks arch her
back as the bundle strains
earth to heaven.
A reflection

in her pond like cattails
waiting for dragonflies. She
grew up in Springfield, a humid
place, a factor in her
affinity to pile high her
findings like a cocoon.

Piano Sonata in B minor
floats over her fence. She
grunts and tries to hum.

Layers

After *Christina's World* by Andrew Wyeth

Her useless legs to her left side, she drags herself over wind-worn
rocks. Tibetan prayer flags tangle above her. The young woman of
cropped, black hair with wisps pulled by the wind is adorned in a
woven sweater, onyx with fuchsia mums and accents of opal and
jade. Her amber eyes wrestle with the stones to see the pinnacle
shrouded by icy sky. She imagines a god assists her in the trek.
Mount Kailash from its gold face watches the woman prostrate
on rough ground with her left hand forward and her right arm
behind. From this mountain abode, the god of the quartz face
measures her body. He weaves clothing, plum like lotus petals.
A shroud created for her crystalline shoulders. She gasps, still as a
carved statue, as a snow leopard balances on a patch of ice before
her. The leopard grasps a blanket, mesh with stars, dwelling in his
jaws. *I bring a cosmic gift from the lapis lazuli face of the mountain,* he
says. The native sun turns amethyst and the nine snow layers of
the mountain become harmonious emerald. The young woman
accepts the gift. *I will spread this carpet on the path around the lake
and the mountain. Please come with me,* she says. A monk passes,
wearing mystic clothing woven of outer nettle stem. The snow
leopard tells her of a ruby dwelling place where gods dye thread
of madder, indigo, and sorrel in large vats. The yak wool is carded,
spun, dyed, and woven. A plum shawl heaps beside her like
hourglass sands. Wrapping it around the door of her bony body,
she thanks the gods. Here Milarepa once glided on the sun's rays
to the mountain top to stop the wrath. The snow leopard guides
her clockwise upon the refined path.

Sacred Hoop

Petroglyph whale emerges
with lightning snake inside.
What are these memories?
Select a thread, lick the tip
right through the eye
up, down, pierce cotton fabric
repair the tear in my dress.

My friends heard the rain
a thousand-year rain
droplets not pricking the skin.
We fetched smooth stones
from rushing waters,
radial pattern on uneven ground.

Asked permission of the plant
before plucking leaves.
Struck a match.
Bundled white sage
smoked, crackled.
Vision blurred
in purification scent.

Stepping into the stitched circle,
chose west quadrant—
The Way of the Teacher.
Beneath my feet
coast live oak dug deep roots
slender and pointed acorns
with thin cap.

Our sacred circle guarded by a warrior.
She chanted to eagle, deer, and bear
toward the four winds—
above, on, below the earth.

What did the shaman see?

I held a wrapped stone sought wisdom.
God said my path is clear.
I am already on it.
Mended by earth and sky
inside the Medicine Wheel.

Sun Dawns Yellow Daisy in a Field of Dead Grasses

love me, love me not raw cut stalk
of lemongrass grinds with fresh turmeric
fragrant and tart I look
for Freya's cloak of feathers

Body in Dumpster

A woman drifts through her dream
house under slant moon.
Built when perfecting
doors and sanding columns held
the signature of the maker.
Hand-painted tiles of birch
trees border the fireplace. Hardwood
floors creak under her vintage movements.
A thud outside. She slips into damp
vines, investigates behind the house.
A woman gasps at the body
folded
thrust into a trash bag.

Library Chair

Burgundy brocade with fleur-de-lis, curved arms trimmed in gold
Holds her and Stephanie, the fiery cat. She pores over
Rapunzel of golden hair.
Hers is dark brown. A long braid
Hangs to her waist.
Dreams
Of escaping this castle.
Twelve-foot stone walls circle a moat.
(She made up the moat.)
Ten years old, no siblings,
She longs to touch orange blossoms beyond the fortress—
To make friends with trolls and ghosts,
Maybe a magician or two.
Inside, a full library to explore.
Thinks the chair reads over her shoulder and climbs
The polished cherry ladder. Each morning
A new book appears.
Today, she sings:
Red book, blue book
Which will it be?
Magic chair
Pick one for me.

Quince

A cell spins around another
as family members give opinions.
She breaks out of the disorder
at 5 a.m. for options at clusters
of wholesale stores on burnt,
cracked sidewalks.

A better price on decorations,
suits, dresses for the quinceañera.
He better not show up on her day.

She scorns the fake tiara. Imagines
herself dancing in the white ball gown—
a wedding dress with beads. Walks
outside wobbling in discounted

stilettos for the waltz.
Cells move to the wound where
he stabbed her heart. She eats
street tacos with a side of cactus.

It Is Winter between the Inhale and the Exhale

The Inuit man got quiet to prepare so he could stop the poison. Cancer took one breast from his wife. He astral-traveled to Greenland. The Vikings knew about *Angelica* for cancer. It is winter between the inhale and the exhale. His wife recedes like seeds hidden from the cold. My friend tried a mushroom cure and it worked. She's known as the goddess of a city and is convincing. *Women's voices frighten them,* Malala said. I got paid less than a man for the same work. This is how it happened. There've been so many Edwards. The first one was a cruel pagan lord. A group of ladies brought Hawaiian quilts. The first pattern inspired by a breadfruit tree casting shadows on a piece of cloth. An echo-style appliqué design of bold colors on white using hand-stitches to hold paradise together. I told the woman I don't do traditional quilting and realized she wasn't asking me that. The overturned truck released an oil spill on Highway 5. Combustion, the stoppage of a city. Follow the way of the White Buffalo Woman. She placed her sacred mind into all people. She brought fire without end and taught them how to walk like a living prayer. They touched heaven and earth with smoke.

Erasure

Twenty stories up a young
Batman lifts his mask to reveal
one

eye. Spies
a green rose, blue stem.

Walks under the horse's head,
ears

a lamp.
Looks across the hard
hats who carry encoded
iron

bars with certain
words erased.

II.

Roots, Weeds, and Soil

Oracle

I visit the Black Madonna in a thin place,
the margin of heaven and earth.

In a vision I sink through a portal
of metallic sides, skewed angles,
and unearth a carved oracle bone—
human, with tiger teeth and a leopard tail.

Then, huge, burning rocks explode
into the midnight sunset.
Forget the night.

The next morning,
clouds like pearls hover
over the blue, spiral staircase.
I dizzy my way down.

Top Hat & Pocket Watch

A white rabbit bounded across the road in front of me and disappeared into an oleander thicket. *Did you see a little girl in a taffeta dress and a clock?* Jefferson Airplane is making a comeback. Life is about to get really weird. Rabbit spirit, like White Buffalo Woman, means good luck. I watched a video from *The Matrix* telling Neo to follow the white rabbit. He noticed a tattoo on her shoulder. *Don't follow her into a hole. Ears up or down?* I don't remember. Wonderland awaits. Good fortune. You are heading in the right direction. A symbol of fertility and desire. I'm in trouble. Buy White Rabbit candy at the Chinese store. Immaculate Conception?

Upon Turning Thirty

The sound of rushing water
reminded me of a poem
I wrote about my daughter.
She was in my womb.
Ocean sprayed in La Jolla
spitting on beach.
We heard sounds
of smashing waves and there
was a salt shaker. Lester the frog
croaked in a chorus,
summer is here again,
at Del Rosa and Lynwood.
My neighbors
watered their grass twice a day.
Everyone else had yards turning
brown while theirs slurped green
like a thorn in my side.

Indigo Child

I.

I sort of told
the nomad I sensed angel
wings between my shoulder
blades. Wings iced with indigo
feathers. At one point,
they unfurled,
filled the room. Then compacted
and I lay down. Covered in a woven wool
blanket. Gong shivered bones.

Candles flickered. The nomad asked,
Can I select an Indigo Angel card for you?
She shuffled, paused, and slid out
a card. The image of an angel with blue
wings reflected in the fluttered
flame. *You have ancient wisdom.*

II.

I can't remember
the first time redwoods
surrounded me. My feet rooted
in pine-needled earth.
Old growth musk. Wind
rushed wild through branches
like waves. Fire scorched
tips. Cones sparked.

The eagle and raven silent.
Only a Swainson's thrush tied
to a stake sang.

Sleep

A night messenger
of bones adorned
in a tattered
dress approaches me
with smooth Stones
clacking in her hands

The spirit explains
marble streaks
vein the Stones
as Stone People
language

By my bedside
light shimmers
through a crystal bowl
and markings in agates

Becomes a story
of Stone People
created
to hold the world together
through roots, weeds,
and soil

A world
of roots,
weeds, and bones

Womb-Door

I.

The idea of being known
Successful
People have expectations
Perceptions
Like a seedling pushing
Through dry earth
Cracks
Feels wind for the first time
Rain pulls the fragile
Leaf
Down. Going backward into the
Ground.
Ice cold, damp, split
Footprint breathes close
Reach to the sun
Afraid to return to who I was
No voice among the murmurs
Invisible
People have expectations
Perceptions

II.

Quiet
Still
Breathe deep.
Pause
Moment
Breathe in sky—
Breathe out clouds.

Walk
Listen
Chant

After a time of frost,
The first bud reaches
Skyward

III.

The leaf hovers over the ground
Bees approach the flower
Click
Plant introduced
Unique
Beautiful
Left womb of ground
Reaching arc of sky
Community
Solitude
Clarity

IV.

The chive has
Hollow leaves.
Both leaves and flowers
Edible

Peeling

There is a message
in this change
in this remove—

bones strong
lie on the mud
stretches
to one weed,
ripping out root.

I Cut My Hair

shorter, something I've wanted to do
for a long time and my hairdresser
suggested it

Did you lose a golf ball?
No, I'm looking for gophers

III.

Body Contains

Living Inside Alchemy

He leaves his friends to wander
Walks on stilts
Searches for a new way
To see a granite spiny lizard
Listens
Peninsular bighorn sheep
High above on rocky gorges
Sand in his skin

This sojourner loses everything
Follows the trail of Matchbox cars
Trusting funds to a stranger
His dream seems so distant
Delay
He sells well-worn lamps
Brings light
To this sacred geometry

A new friend appears unexpected
Like blinding winds
He roams beyond her breath
Under crocheted clouds
Longs
Yearns to find answers
In the Murray Canyon
Beside the crackle of blue fire

Reflections

Words spoken by green
skeleton
dwelling at the base

of the Giant Fig
echo through
his thin rib spaces.

Flamingo, Masai
giraffe, and
impala listen

drinking from alka-
line, saline
Lake Manyara.

I fished in a
boat and saw
a mermaid splash and

swim to the shoreline.
Mami Wata
combed curly, black hair

gazing into the mirror
as a snake
wrapped around her.

I perched my boat.
Snake stared.
Mami smiled, leaving

behind gems and watches.
Good fortune!
I am a rich man.

Watermama came
as a dream
demanded her jewels

returned. Her terms:
Agree to
be faithful and you

stay wealthy. Refuse
and become
ill. I dried up in this

tree cave, her shrine.
Bells, candles,
statuary, yams,

palm wine, and my skull—
sacrificed,
an earthly death

under frayed, red-
white banner
and fig blossom hiss.

Corpse Candles All

His eyebrows
narrowed
to a
thin
line. His smile exposed by
a pinstripe shirt, Orchid Summer
lipstick
his chunky teeth

Do you want grapefruits?
I have thousands. Because
of my medications, I cannot
taste their juice.

Conversations

The Ceiling creaked
Grave Rubbings for a quilt

Five footsteps tapped like a drum
part of his Dress

I thought you were in the Attic
The Hawk gazed down from the phone pole

I was going to talk
flapping her wings

with you
dissolved

Shape the Clay

> We shape clay to birth a vessel, yet it's the hollow within
> that makes it useful.
>
> —*Tao Te Ching*, Lao Tzu

The lone maple leaf on the driveway begins
to turn yellow and brown,
forms a leaf cup like curling fingers
on the front seat of my car.
I think about how vessels have empty
space enclosed
by a thin surface of veins.

Wind and heat present like a friend,
never alone in flash floods,
this dark valley where clouds explode
in giant plumes, lit edges.
I wonder about a boat of chipped paint
sunk on the desert floor,
ghost family damp from rains.

Antlers dip in wax half-moon up the wall.
Eyes stare. Two ravens
have watercolor conversations as they arch
over my head, ignore my pulse.
I grasp glass bones formed in flame, coiled
with rope, war wounds,
transparent runes as body contains.

Yarn Bombing

I crochet. The web grows
encasing my cigarette smoke
near the burnt-out shelter—

Would you live in
a house of granny squares?
I was not made to dwell
in the desert, once

a place of salt.

Clay heads whisper to me:
Jump in front of the train.

I might consider
if I knew their names. The sweater
unravels as Beguines'
needles click

knit one
purl two

knitting a cocoon around
the basement pillar. Bees
drone in woolly torch

flowers. You discuss the
weather with them. Hospice
nurse massages

my mother's
pale hands, scarred wrists,
Yarn-bomb her trunk and branches.
I negotiate this trend.

Lady of Holiness

After Sabina Lampadius

As a symbol
of life and death,
I, Nerthus,
Earth Mother,
bear the
cycle in a seed until
the plant
decays home.
I dwell
in island birch trees,
sacred grove.
My carriage
veiled
with a woolen
vestment
touched by one
priest.
I am
land, ocean,
roots,
virgin forests,
lakes, and
ancient bones.

Let Us Keep This Story False

Flight canceled.

I can take the train to Newark.

Write my
Fifteenth book about
Graveyards

Heavenly

> To live in a body is to experience fragmentation.
>
> —Jacques Lacan

She was his starlet—
soft curls, satin dress.
Dreams burned
in the crossbeam. Meera,
spooled in a saffron sari, paisley pattern,
Krishna's beloved,
swayed under the flowing tent
of turmeric color depicting
a central, black medallion.

Fig-figure, Celeste
fig

White moth orchid
slowly grew loose
clusters of blossoms.
She tapped the metal singing
bowl for an infinite
sound. Shelves of African
fertility goddesses,
carved wood
like her grandma collected.
No one craved their evidence
after Grandma died.

Wires wrapped around Meera's wrists
as she designed a mandala
of burgundy and green seeds. The tree
house over-

looked the ancient lake
of leafless addictive medicine
that didn't affect her that way.

IV.

She-Child Stories

Who Would Ever Hug the Trash Man?

The dog barks from 11 p.m. to midnight trying to figure out why
people gather to burn the sky in pops & crackles. *(I need to sleep.)*
Andy kidnaps his son when he is five in a rusted truck. City lost
to farms, dwindles to an abandoned shack. Wolves live here.
Wolf was the first creature to experience death. Like crusts of
bread, his son eats opiates as they drop on the floor. Ants of
illusion. Ants spread out the earth for people to live upon. This is
not collectable quality. Volume 12, Number Five, August 1993.
Tom & Mable travel to Africa where they did not photograph
anything at first, overwhelmed by a new land. Turning their garage
into a studio. *Are you setting up a darkroom? A digital darkroom.*
My daughter still uses film—I never thought Kodak would be obsolete.
You have at least ten trash bags stuffed with recyclables (you
begin to fill another) tied to one grocery cart. *Good morning,*
you smile. The woman says my art has inspired her. She wants
to make a book of pastel meditations. I used to lead a women's
circle. Last week I saw them & know I cannot rejoin them. Why
do I long, mourn for past ashes? On July 20, three years later,
something significant happens. Cops return the boy to his mom.
Andy dies without dignity & his son believes in God. *(Forgiveness*
tastes sour.) Behind the stopped garbage truck, voices chatter.
I see a young girl run down the driveway. She gives a gift of two
bottled waters & receives a big hug from the trash man (mask
over face). Her family looks on, laughing. She forgets the smell.
Sweat drips down my cheek.

Meltwaters

I.

You follow her,
jump up,
a car bumps your
thick fur.

II.

The ghosts of ants parade
the grout core line
spreading at the hollow rug
fringe. Their thirst remains.

III.

In another life—
ice under paws,
breath steams.
Not crunching
date
palm seeds.

IV.

Banana leaf basket
on river drifting.
She thanks
the goddess of water,
the candle bows
and vanishes.

V.

Blue eyes,
stark thoughts
of a barefoot home.
Your saliva speaks
a language she does not
understand.

Telling the Old Stories

A blackbird rested in your hand.

Long ago, Wolf reigned over a kingdom of clans. *We need a recordkeeper and storyteller,* said Wolf. Someone to write the she-stories. He howled across the night sky of the eighth moon. Shooting star burned at Wolf's feet. A she-child lay curled as tiny flames leapt off her skin. Wolf offered a prayer of thanksgiving to the sky goddess. If you listen carefully in the forest, you can hear the she-child's stories where wolves establish their dens.

Molten

Molten saline water explodes to the surface
in circles through stone.
Life on Mars?

She descends cut stone, no mortar, and angle changes,
into the stepwells.
Water is a person.

I see Mandarin characters on the side of the gray bowl
in a tiny stall.
I lived in Taiwan.

Piles of framed pictures jumble on the floor. He grabs
a sliding print.
This is from Japan.

His grin reveals a missing front tooth. Immigrant
from Shanghai.
Ancestral home.

My daughter has been there and liked it, I tell him.
He can barely understand.
Xiexie (thank you). Xiexie ni.

Imagine

Her sword pierces
the moon.
Teeth dyed black,
she ascends.
Imagines a lake
on ice,

too cold
for her puma.
She hurls
a storm. Splits earth.
Slices adobe walls
of chipped, aqua paint.
Inside, a mother
weaves

pine needle baskets,
lingering scent,
for a stranger.

Messages

Sybil writes prophecies inside her cave on blue oak leaves.
Markers of home. This junction between the underworld and
mortals in the deep time.

Vintage leather suitcase open like a mouth, accepts
ten dollar bills cast inside like autumn leaves.
Do you always dress like a fortune-teller? he asks.
The keys on the Brother typewriter tap-tapa-tap
prophetic words on a 3x5 postcard. Strike out
the mistakes. She learns to type in high school.
Practices at home on her mother's black metal
Smith-Corona. Her kids master typing at an old
mahogany desk using a computer program
and a keyboard.

A holy wanderer comes to ask about his future. Bones scrape
on slick mosses as Sybil reaches for a carved, notched leaf.

Memory Pockets

You explained the difference between Tibetan and Zen
Buddhism and could pronounce the name of the author of my
daily devotional on mindfulness. You spoke the name of the
coffeehouse we worked at as teens, "Nexus"—a word buried
in pockets of memory. You turned out to be a good cook. I served
tables as glass coffee cups chinked. Helped the overdosed. You are
still in touch with a friend I barely knew. He has a family. His name
brings back days at Westport—India prints, incense, and black
light posters. You spent the past two year's caretaking your
mom who still knows your name, but needs others' full-time care.
I wonder if she remembers me, the little girl from up the street
with dark eyes and black hair? I was careful because your dad
was a cop.

V.

Bendable Bones

Corpse Candle

The cow munched the red
dress with white daisies,
her favorite.

She crunched between grave
stones. A small one,
curved top was

incised with *Mary*.
Five years old, like her.
Rumor said a dim

light floated above
the brittle ground from
this spot to Mary's

home and back again
the night before the
accident. Mother wrestled

the cow for a shred of memory,
fraying the left cap sleeve.
Dianthus scent in clumps
sprinkled on the mound.

What She Learned about Death

Wax sings upright

prism
the sagging
sun

Sacred Words

The moon is fourteen parts
of darkness. In the fourteenth
of the gates of light, I write
sacred words on clay shards.
A song of the sage poured out
onto stone. This ritual
from the vault of heaven
as the sun ascends.

Water stills.

A green beetle. The kind that buzzes
into the nest of your hair. Iridescent
armor dives into the coffee
cup. *Splash*. Tries to climb, bobbing
liquid edges. I grab the handle,
and flick the cup.
Beetle zips away, not stopping
to say thank you.

Receptors

Scraping
behind the bathroom
Mirror. The rat
wonders if the
Nest
eclipses the sun?

Corpse Candle II

After Adriana Salazar

Dead crow stitched with nylon
strings Moved like a marionette
Eyes pierced Indigo wings enveloped

Device
Rhythm
Motor stretched

Cemetery plants
waltzed

She pruned plastic
leaves Kept her
distance He moved
to another padded
chair

Green Leather Club Chairs

Under the overpass,

a fire dissolved

the sofa—clothes in its arms

like a hearth.

He heard their voices.

Languages are dying.

Stories disappear.

A Burial

Miscarriage, five months—
Caged womb still bloated
From her star child.
She collapses on the tile
Floor, heaves a flood
Of tears, and tastes salt.
Unimagines the nursery.
Facing friends. Facing herself.

She views the room through eyeglass lenses
Linked together like a wall. Her vision
Skews the lamp. Husband a shadow.
He enters the branched
Door.

Their daughter,
Of dusk and dawn,
Now a circle of tiny,
Bendable bones
Wearing ice wings.

Sybil

Sybil's skeleton contained in a statue of the winged deer.
The daily bell stopped. She wanted to know flight.

Blue head of a lioness,
She clutches a scepter in one hand,
An ankh by her side in the other.
Slim, red skirt matches
The solar disc circled
By two cobras crowning her.
Thick, black hair drapes
A blouse the color of her skin.
Her body contains waters
Of the sky—moisture, rain, air.

Water is a goddess.

VI.
From Earth from Caves

How to See-Speak Art

After Wendy Xu

You must allow art to be your voice. You must not
think all people will like it. You will find a mentor to push
you to create larger, add folds, or experiment
with materials. This is a journey to my heart
the heart of the sacred fig where
are your eyes? This is because you bring your overlay
to my story and I have explained that to you. You must suspect
art has one answer when it is not
so simple. I stitch together fabrics
and listen for them to tell me
the next step. A hawk flies
overhead encouraging me to explore the land. An ancient
tree loses its leaves
choked out by other figs. Wait
I promise you will experience something new. You and I
grasp a fabric painting in our timeless moment.

Passion & Tangles

After Ruth Ellen Kocher

blue heron spread its wings across Lake Evans
you find a heart carved in
Montezuma bald cypress
tough rough skin

I might say this tree is sacred
worshipped by natives in Mexico

spiral leaves
canopy of branches
cypress knees for roots

fishing line almost strangles
mallard duck
you would never say men originate from rocks or ocelots

I'm thinking the Cahuilla hunted
game at Fairmount Park before horse-drawn
wagons
dipped buckets
in the clear stream

did you know
ancestors originated from earth from caves
trees to jaguars into people

he didn't seem upset to cut the thick branch
arching over the lake
framing snow-covered mountains

carousel gone families gather for car show, bbq
we share the desire to keep this park clean

Gates

River overflows

I slip as ice chunks
t
o
p
p
l
e
tombstones

Almost Super Moon

You carry questions in a mended deerskin pouch that once held
the warmth of the sun pulled through a hole in the sky around
your neck. Each one on a slip of paper. People say they don't
believe in words from a cookie. Cracked open, they hope for riches
or romance. Between night and dawn, your paper asks out loud,
Where will you search for intimacy? The placard stares on the side of
the polished Ford truck, *Juan Diaz, President.* Forgotten lawn
mower rests on the pavement. I ran for president in sixth grade.
Don't we all want to be seen? Made artistic signs. VOTE FOR ME
to change the world. Soon I would not be able to outrun the boys.
I search street edges and discover a raven feather turning white to
black because he stole the sun from the Old Man and released it.
In eventide the sun moves far to the right horizon limit and
descends behind hazy mountains. Summer constellations chant
prayers, wander, and return. This night Big Dipper pours into an
almost super moon. Angry mobs flood the streets. Their homes
buried to disguise urban renewal profits. Monsoon walks over
dead bodies in the holy site. Still, you try to warn raven as his nest
of twigs crashes with the falling tree. Watch the untamed toddler
plummet four stories. You do not want to meet creatures from
outer space. Polaris does not move. The earth rotates as Coyote
flings stars along the way.

Eat or We Both Starve

Extensive sanctuary system
littered with whalebones,
self adhesive. Cheetah's breath
could meet my own? Tenth life
for a big cat.

A world of nomads hear
music. Flora is essential as treasure
to her heirs. The illustrated woman
still scans the horizon
for enemies.

Confident that the melting
sea does not have lunch
for a month

Ideal Pet Companion

The bat can listen to itself as a navigational vector.

—Roy Wagner

Echolocation. The sounds of the hero speaking bounced off eucalyptus bark and greenschist stones. She listened for the return vibrations and walked in safety.

Nocturnal. The hero appreciated the bat as a miniature dragon—a symbol for happiness, transition, rite of passage. Facing her fears of the dark, the hero died to the need to be important. Bat helped her let go of desire for a title.

Sonar. The hero searched to find her tribe. Sonar from bat's nose gave her perfect navigation. The hero was not lost in the night. Alert to the noises of animals prowling.

Curls Dyed Gray

Sofa cushions wheezed under
Two, young sentinels. Their eyes
Stared through my forehead, hands
Perched on their thighs. Dust

Spat as they leaned, grabbed, stacked
Clacking, restacked a tower of
Books—

Small tight ball of fur darted, zigzagged,
Barking as the women, one blond
Of soft waves, the other, side buzzed,
Curls dyed gray cracked

Open torn edges, pointed mid-page, *aspects*
The other poked, *deep*   woof
Grabbed a slice of pages,
Stabbed   woof   *mystical*
Spiritual of attitude   woof

Inner
Voice

Flipped pages   woof   *The anima, who*
Can initiate a man   woof   *into the mystery*
Of his own   woof   *feminine being*
Is projected

Woof   Pages clapped open   woof

Lover
The wolf

Sea Ice

After Life in the Poles: Waiting for the Ice to Break Up
by Christopher Ulivo

Sand and rocks sink
beneath their feet
A silence only the sea
can understand
Clouds reflect
crayon colors. Snow
islands, spoke in code
of knocking bones
against sediment cliffs
Did they dare
venture out in their
small,
wooden boat—
the sail in tatters?
Paleo-Indian child
climbs into the boat
Watches the sea
split into puzzle
pieces. Ocean black
cracks and breaks
Her burnt bones hold
a handle covered
in seal skin
She strikes
the driftwood rim
of caribou skin
drum and sings an
ayaya. *Spring sun come soon*
Sail away
under first full moon

The woman sings
Bloom fireweed
Monkshood, Larkspur
Arctic lupine from seed
Biting wind
capsizes the fishing
boat once a place of cast
gillnets
haunted salmon

Farewell

There was a type of leaving, candle snuffed out, cursive smoke.
In agreement,

Two stayed grieving beneath the peeled eucalyptus. Knit bodies to
The earth, dripped

Wax. The corpse candles revealed their death walks.

VII.

She Buried the Moon

(non-linear narratives)

Lies

Stone Woman remembered

Running from her father into

A cave. He told her

Never to come out

Or she would die.

She believed
His words.

She buried
The moon.

He wanted a hunter for

A child. Yelled every day,

You are worth no more than a stone.
Get out of my sight.

He chased her

Into this cave. She became

Stone like the alabaster

Walls.

Upon Wondering Why No One Came to Find Her

She asked:
Where is the Desert Tribe?
My mother?
My best friend who can touch cholla unstung?

Father tells them I am dead
Eaten by a mountain lion.

Threads of Fate

After the stellar lights arched around Polaris—

I visioned an antlered dog sniffing
Across the black
Stone's edge. Sliding around
Gray, striped icebergs. The hound strained,
The staff of wood, basket shape in the top,
Was gripped in his jaw.

The earth
Groaned.

Winds stung,
Sung a haunting
Water spirit song.

This hound found the crone

Buried in ice. He remembered her
Touch,
Hands spinning silken thread. I learned
To weave a shawl of navy blue and white
Long ago in steady rhythm,
Back and forth.

The Mosaic goddess said
She had chanted:
The death of the gods,
A world under water,
And the world resurfacing fertile and new.
Back and forth.

Requiem

Bird-man stood in a stupor at the shoreline.
The air after-a-storm crisp. He could see a ship

boosting strange sails. *I promised to protect
you,* Bird-man said to the gentle waves.

Watching the expanse before him, sadness
drenched him because of his missing bird-egg-child.

Bird-woman languished behind him and
gestured in slow circular movements. *It is not

your fault,* she said. *This is still our child.*
Bird-man held her close. His hands moved

in the rhythm of the waves. He said to Yemoja,
*You are the mother of all fish. Please take

our child into your care.* Bird-man guided
Bird-woman in the endless walk to the cave.

What is this? she asked. Bird-man said,

*The shadow-soul-spirit of a human twin who
has died.* Bird-woman said, *We must bury

this tender shadow.* After three days, Bird-
man carved a grave in the cold cave floor.

Bird-woman sprinkled water and
chanted, *May the road be open to you.*

*May nothing evil meet you on your way.
May you find the road good when you go

in peace.* Listless, Bird-woman thought of her
lost child. Fish and cowries were dropped

into the grave. The silver fish from the sea
spoke, *All is not lost. You think you are alone*

in the day and in the darkness of night.
Under the new moon, a mermaid

of dark, flowing hair and wide eyes tenderly
placed a bird-egg-child on the rippled shore.

Bird-Man Courts Bird-Woman

Each language has different eyes sitting inside its words.

—Herta Muller

Bird-man struggled. A wiggling silver
fish tried to escape from his orange beak.

He had dove 30 feet, wings tight, to capture
this salty morsel. The silver fish from the sea

spoke, *you will imagine death in this ocean.*
Bird-man puffed up his black crest and strutted

circles around her—the Bird-woman.
The other royal terns tussled to delay him

with clear shrills as the sea spray stung his
eyes. She accepted his offering, but she wrangled

to swallow the prize. Another woman clashed
into her and stole the fish. Still, she found

him desirable. Perhaps she would mate
with him in this secret colony, not returning

to the honking horns of the Nigerian
shore. Her thoughts sifted like sign language

behind her back. His hands folded and turned
in conflicted signals. Would she stay?

Hunted

The darkened sun fell through the clouds.

Cool water slid down his parched throat.
Same water poured in solo
Purification rites,
Thrown on hot rocks, sacred
Steam.

I visioned a goddess
Of turquoise Mosaic ice tiles.

I desired to touch
Her color like deep,
Glacial pools. Once I stood
On a glacier cutting earth.

The antlered dog
Hunted her scent.

The Sound of One Hand

Bird-man and Bird-woman chased young blue
crabs in short shallow dives cracking shells.

I am with child, said Bird-woman.
Bird-man gouged a hole in the sand

for her to nest. He stood with wings arched
over her resting body. *I will protect you,*

he said by twisted hand motions
in circles cutting through salt air.

She strained her hands upwards and flickered
his thoughts. Inside her womb the unborn

transformed from fish to bird-egg-child.
Bird-woman bore a buff spotted egg.

A large gull swooped swift as air
in tunnels of disappearance to steal

the tern yolk. *Kree, kree, kree,*
shouted the sickened

Bird-woman. Stern-faced Bird-man
looped to thump the predator.

Guarded his egg.
A month stretched

like a delayed moon cycle. Storming winds
howled and shifted direction as Olokun

stirred the dark, turbulent depths of his swollen
ocean. Waves crashed. A swell washed

this egg into the sea. Panic dissolved
the night. Only a pouch remained

on Bird-woman's breast.
A crossed-out language of bones.

Carved Story

Humanity denied her mirrored truth.

They attempted to stop time,
Even death. Their story carved in runes
On her silver amulet chair
Made of stump.

The crone glanced up to see lights of viridian
Like agates shape-shifted made of stars.

Revealed the silhouette of her antlered dog.

The Language of Rain

Pat-a-pat
Rain began to fall

Revealing secrets
Of the Medicine Wheel

Water seeped into her cave
She
Imagined
Her
Outer
Shell

Crumbled

Acknowledgments

I am grateful to the publications, in which the following poems, sometimes in different versions, first appeared.

Artemis Journal: "Passion & Tangles"

BlogNostics Peu Verset micropoetry: "Peeling," "Let Us Keep This Story False," "Receptors," "I Cut My Hair," "Green Leather Club Chairs," "Gates," "What She Learned about Death"

Cactus Heart Press: "Yarn Bombing"

Cadence Collective: "Corpse Candle," "Eat or We Both Starve," "Top Hat & Pocket Watch"

Driftwood Press: "Indigo Child," "Molten"

East Jasmine Review: "Conversations," "Corpse Candles All"

Eternal Haunted Summer: "Lady of Holiness"

Indiana Voice Journal: "Womb-Door," "Curls Dyed Gray," "Memory Pockets"

Lyre Lyre: "Almost Super Moon"

Muddy River Poetry Review: "Oracle"

Phantom Seed: "Living Inside Alchemy"

Poetry Quarterly: "Savory"

Revolution House: Who Would Ever Hug the Trash Man?"

Rose Red Review: "A Ritual"

Spectrum: An Anthology of Southern California Poets: "Meltwaters"

The Honest Ulsterman: "Upon Turning Thirty," "Sacred Words"

The Lake: "How to See-Speak Art"

The MOON Magazine: "It Is Winter between the Inhale and the Exhale"

The Poetry Bus: "Quince"

The Sand Canyon Review: "Body in Dumpster"

three drops from a cauldron: "Imagine"

Tin Cannon #1: "Library Chair"

Twelve Winters Press: "Reflections"

Wild Lemon Project: "Sacred Hoop"

Young Ravens Literary Review: "Sea Ice"

Zoomoozophone Review: "Corpse Candle II"

Many thanks to Jessica Morey-Collins for your support and poem-a-day; Ivonne Gordon, who encourages me to look at the world in new ways; Katia Hage for inspiration beyond the seen; Siri Ajeet Kaur for spending time with my poetry; Larry Eby, who encourages me to try new things; Michael Cooper for his insights and for believing in me; KL Straight and Bory Thach for their wise input; PoetrIE for their edits; Dan Rinne for his help and support; and many friends and strangers who inspire my lines.

Cover artwork, "Refuge" by Cindy Rinne; author photo by Natalie Valdez; cover and interior book design by Diane Kistner; Legacy Sans text and Macondo titling

About FutureCycle Press

FutureCycle Press is dedicated to publishing lasting poetry books, chapbooks, and anthologies in the English language, in both print-on-demand and Kindle ebook formats. Founded in 2007 by long-time independent editor/publishers and partners Diane Kistner and Robert S. King, the press incorporated as a nonprofit in 2012. A number of our editors are distinguished poets and writers in their own right, and we have been actively involved in the small press movement going back to the early seventies.

The FutureCycle Poetry Book Prize and honorarium is awarded annually for the best full-length volume of poetry we publish in a calendar year. Introduced in 2013, our Good Works projects are anthologies devoted to issues of universal significance as well as other efforts in support of poets and writers—with all proceeds donated to a related worthy cause. Our Selected Poems series highlights contemporary poets with a substantial body of work to their credit; with this series we strive to resurrect work that has had limited distribution and is now out of print.

We are dedicated to giving all of the authors we publish the care their work deserves, making our catalog of titles the most diverse and distinguished it can be, and paying forward any earnings to fund more great books.

We've learned a few things about independent publishing over the years. We've also evolved a unique, resilient publishing model that allows us to focus mainly on vetting and preserving for posterity poetry collections of exceptional quality without becoming overwhelmed with bookkeeping and mailing, fundraising activities, or taxing editorial and production "bubbles." To find out more about what we are doing, come see us at www.futurecycle.org.

The FutureCycle Poetry Book Prize

All full-length volumes of poetry published by FutureCycle Press in a given calendar year are considered for the annual FutureCycle Poetry Book Prize. This allows us to consider each submission on its own merits, outside of the context of a contest. Too, the judges see the finished book, which will have benefitted from the beautiful book design and strong editorial gloss we are famous for.

The book ranked the best in judging is announced as the prizewinner in the subsequent year. There is no fixed monetary award; instead, the winning poet receives an honorarium of 20% of the total net royalties from all poetry books and chapbooks the press sold online in the year the winning book was published. The winner is also accorded the honor of being on the panel of judges for the next year's competition; all judges receive copies of all contending books to keep for their personal libraries.